Glitter That Was Once Gold

Long Island Gold Coast Trivia

© Copyright 2005 Kevin Durst
All rights reserved. No part of this publication may be reproduced, stored in a retrieval system, or transmitted, in any form or by any means, electronic, mechanical, photocopying, recording, or otherwise, without the written prior permission of the author.

Note for Librarians: a cataloguing record for this book that includes Dewey Decimal Classification and US Library of Congress numbers is available from the Library and Archives of Canada. The complete cataloguing record can be obtained from their online database at:
www.collectionscanada.ca/amicus/index-e.html
ISBN 1-4120-4940-7
Printed in Victoria, BC, Canada

TRAFFORD

Offices in Canada, USA, Ireland, UK and Spain

This book was published *on-demand* in cooperation with Trafford Publishing. On-demand publishing is a unique process and service of making a book available for retail sale to the public taking advantage of on-demand manufacturing and Internet marketing. On-demand publishing includes promotions, retail sales, manufacturing, order fulfilment, accounting and collecting royalties on behalf of the author.

Book sales for North America and international:
Trafford Publishing, 6E–2333 Government St.,
Victoria, BC v8t 4p4 CANADA
phone 250 383 6864 (toll-free 1 888 232 4444)
fax 250 383 6804; email to orders@trafford.com

Book sales in Europe:
Trafford Publishing (uk) Ltd., Enterprise House, Wistaston Road Business Centre,
Wistaston Road, Crewe, Cheshire cw2 7rp UNITED KINGDOM
phone 01270 251 396 (local rate 0845 230 9701)
facsimile 01270 254 983; orders.uk@trafford.com

Order online at:
www.trafford.com/robots/04-2748.html

10 9 8 7 6 5 4 3 2

For Freddy who stands by me.

For Ann and Derek who traveled with me.

White Eagle approach– Brookville

Introduction

Most of the glitter that was once gold on Long Island is gone, but some still remains hidden.

During the late 1800's through the early 1900's, Long Island was the backdrop for architectural extravagances and reckless spending for luxuries that were characteristic of the period referred to the "Gilded Age" or the "Age of Elegance". It was a time when American tycoons had big money, no taxation and were vying with one another for prevalence.

When I first moved to Long Island, I was thrilled by what I saw, opulent estates like Old Westbury Gardens, Falaise and Eagles Nest. But I was led to believe there were so many more. I wanted to create a book that would include some of my findings as well as events that happened back then, that has an affect on us today.

Many of these extraordinary mansions are still private homes, some altered, some not. Some were adapted to reuse, and others demolished. Some are open for tours and events and after visiting some of them one will come away with a sense of the grandeur that was so a part of the Gilded Age.

All of Long Island was estate country, but the famed "Gold Coast" was said to have stretched from Great Neck to Huntington on the north shore.

The great and powerful, rich and famous came to Long Island because it was in close proximity to Manhattan, and was also a sportsman's paradise. There were foxhunts and horseback riding in Old Westbury and Wheatley Hills. Yachting and fishing could be found off the coast in Glen Cove, Sands Point, Kings Point, Bayshore and Oakdale. Golfing was popular in Brookville, North Hills and Sayville.

Payne Whitney bought five Long Island farms to form his estate. Whitney was ranked third-richest man in America and when he died in 1927 at his Manhasset estate *Greentree,* Whitney's daughter Joan (Mrs. Charles Shipman Payson) was co-founder of the New York Mets in 1962.

Long Island Power Authority began with politician E. D. Morgan's desire to electrify his 325-acre Wheatley Hills Estate.

Madame Chaing Kai-Shek, widow of the Chinese Nationalist leader moved to a 37-acre Lattingtown estate in 1975 where she lived in seclusion for many years.

John Aldred, who was associated with Gillette Safety Razor Company and W.D. Guthrie together, purchased the 400-acre town of Lattingtown to construct their two self-contained kingdoms. This required demolition of sixty homes and businesses.

During the Long Island estate boom, an estate staff could number anywhere from ten to the hundreds.

Just west of the intersection of Wheatley Road and the north Long Island Expressway service road you will see a wrought iron gate with the name *The Crossroads*. This was once the estate of William Russell Grace and it is where the Prince of Wales played a game of Polo during his visit in 1924.

The second largest private residence in the United States is right in Cold Spring Harbor and was serviced by 125 servants. With 127 rooms, *Oheka*, is second only to George Washington Vanderbilt's *Biltmore* in North Carolina with 250 rooms.

The former home of Benjamin and Alexandra Moore, *Chelsea* in Muttontown was turned into the Nassau County Cultural Development Center at Muttontown on Route 25A. Today, the future of the building is unknown.

Chelsea bridge and moat- Muttontown

CBS founder, William S. Paley and his wife Barbara Mortimer Paley, resided at an 81-acre North Hills estate named *Kiluna Farms*. This estate earned distinction as the site of the largest residential burglary on Long Island. Thieves made off with $184,000.00 in jewelry.

The Long Island mansions were often modeled after the great houses of Europe and in some cases, the whole rooms were imported. Europe had historic buildings and royal titles, both of which were very desirable to America's nouveau rich. Europe needed money and America's "royalty" had it.

On Meudon Road off Frost Creek Road in Lattingtown you can see a group of pillars perched on top of a hill, and wrought iron fencing in the area. These are the remnants of the W.D Guthrie estate, *Meudon*. Guthrie was lawyer to the Standard Oil Rockefellers.

It is estimated that half of the mansions built during the Gilded Age were demolished during the 1950's and 1960's because they were deserted and vandalized.

Chelsea Fountain - Muttontown

Chelsea, the former Benjamin Moore estate on 25A in Muttontown contains an unusual fountain with faces that once sprayed water from their mouths into a center pool. Mr. Moore was the grandson of Clement Clark Moore, author of "T'was The Night Before Christmas".

Burrwood, the home of Walter Jennings, a director of Standard Oil, once stood at Jennings Field in Lloyd Harbor.

Lands End on Hoffstot Lane in Sands Point was the inspiration for the home of Tom and Daisy Buchanan's home in the <u>Great Gatsby</u>. The home was built in 1902 for Herbert Bayard Swope, editor of The New York World and later owned by the Payson family.

The estate grounds of Harrison and Mona Williams is now the Bayville housing development named *Oak Point* after the original estate that contained an indoor aviary housing more than 200 exotic birds.

The grounds of Wall Street chairman Mortimer Schiff's estate (*Norwood*), the Montague Flagg estate (*Applewood*), and John Carver's estate (*Wrexleigh*) now form the Tiffany Creek Hill Preserve in Oyster Bay.

Chelsea – Muttontown

State University at Stonybrook campus was once part of *Sunwood*, the Frank Melville Estate. Melville was president of Melville Shoe Corporation.

Stables – Caumsett – Lloyd Harbor

Scenes from the movie "Arthur" were filmed at the *Caumsett* stables, the Marshall Fields III estate in Lloyd Harbor and the old Martin estate, *The Knole* in Old Westbury.

Woodward Drive in Oyster Bay Cove is named after Robert Woodward owner of *The Playhouse*.

Forker House – Kings Point

Wiley Hall, part of the Merchant Marines Academy in Kings Point, was once the home of Henri Bendel, specialty store founder. The next owner *of Forker House*, as it was named, was Walter Chrysler and his family. Chrysler was founder of Chrysler Corporation and they lived there until their son's death in the estate swimming pool.

Harbor Hill, the 52-room, 640-acre Roslyn estate was owned by radio and telegraph tycoon Clarence Hungerford Mackay. Mr. MacKay was President of companies that would later become International Telephone & Telegraph and Western Union. The wedding present built by his father, John W., was completed in 1905 at a cost of $6,000,000.00.

The turreted gatehouse and wrought iron gates are the only remains of the Alva Vanderbilt Belmont Estate, *Beacon Towers*, in Sands Point   This castle is said to be one of the inspirations for F. Scott Fitzgerald's book <u>The Great Gatsby</u>.

Glen Cove had the first telephone exchange on Long Island.

The Admiralty community just off of Montauk Highway in West Bayshore was originally the estate of philanthropist Langdon Ketchum Thorne.

The Pratt Family, led by Charles Millard Pratt started accumulating some 2,000 acres in Glen Cove. He divided his property among his children, and by 1920 the Pratt Family Complex consisted of 21 estates, with 125 buildings on ¾ of a mile of Glen Cove Sound frontage. The estate group of summer homes is undoubtedly the largest group owned by one family.

Clayton - Roslyn

Clayton, the former residence of Childs Frick is now the home of Nassau County Museum of Fine Arts in Roslyn Harbor. Originally Henry Clay Frick bought the 200-acre estate for his son as a wedding present.

The likeness of three Coe family servants are carved into wooden corbels that extend out from the side of *Coe Hall* overlooking the formal gardens. They are Joe Ebel the chauffer, Henry White the valet, and Tom Dawson who served as tour guide on the Coe's Wyoming ranch.

Coe Hall – Brookville

The facades of *Coe Hall* in Brookville were modeled after several different English manor homes including Moynes Park, Atholhampton and Saint Catherine's Court.

Manhattan banker, Ferdinand Eberstadt, owned *Target Rock Farm* in Lloyd Harbor. The estate was named after the 14-foot boulder in the Long Island Sound that was used as target practice for the British troops during the American Revolution. In 1968 Mr. Eberstadt donated the property as a park to block the Long Island Lighting Company's planned acquisition of the land. The land is now known as Target Rock Refuge.

The Nursery was the Belmont Estate in North Babylon and is now the site of Belmont State Park. 459-acres were donated by Mrs. August Belmont Jr. Near the park, on the Southern State Parkway, you will see a line of old spruce trees which once lined the original driveway to the estate. There are also two cannons that marked the original entrance to the mansion.

Lawyer L. H. Sherman had his estate in North Hills, the current location of Buckley Country Day.

The Seminary of The Immaculate Conception in Lloyd Harbor was once the estate of Illinois-born Ronald Ray Conklin Esq., *Rosemary Farm*. The estate hosted performances by Tyrone Powers, John Phillips Sousa as well as John and Ethel Barrymore in the outdoor amphitheater. The amphitheater contained waterfalls, stone bridges, a grotto and a rising island from the middle of the pond. Instead of a curtain falling, the fountains would shoot up water to mark the end of a performance.

The 769-acre Wildwood Park, off of Landing Road in Wading River, was once a part of two estates. *Wildwood,* was owned by Roland G. Mitchell and *Driftwood Manor,* was owned by Joseph G. Robin, banker and Wall Street investor. Mr. Robin was eventually committed to a sanitarium for his attempted suicides after the media discovered that he was involved with the 1910 stock manipulation of The Northern Bank of New York, of which he was Director and a major shareholder.

Eagle's Nest - Centerport

The estate known as *Eagles Nest*, was owned by railroads' famous family member and president of the New York Central Railroad, W.K. Vanderbilt. Vanderbilt also inaugurated the Vanderbilt Cup Auto Race in 1904 and is responsible for the construction of the Vanderbilt Motor Parkway in 1908. Vanderbilt turned his parkway over to Nassau, Suffolk and Queens Counties in lieu of $80,000 in back taxes. On Easter of 1938 the entire parkway was closed and now exists in only disconnected patches.

Mr. Clarence MacKay, of *Harbor Hill* in Roslyn, never spoke to his daughter after she married a poor immigrant and became Mrs. Irving Berlin. It is rumored that Berlin bailed his father-in-law out when the Depression took its toll on his fortune.

Mr. Harrison Williams, like a few other estate owners would commute from his estate, *Oak Point* (Bayville) to Wall Street on his yacht, "The Whim". The estate's original garage / stable complex are now part of the Village Hall complex.

The inventor of the electric meter, William Barstow, resided in the Spanish-style mansion, *Elm Point*, in Kings Point, now the United States Merchant Marine Academy Museum.

Welwyn, the former Harold Pratt mansion in Glen Cove, was used for the filming of "Age of Innocence" (1992) and "New Leaf" (1971). The mansion is now the Holocaust Center of Nassau County.

Eagle's Nest– Centerport

Hecksher Park, at the end of the Hecksher Parkway, was once the estate of George C. Taylor, an eccentric millionaire. Taylor doubled the fortune that his father, Moses, left him. Mr. Taylor was romantically involved with his head housekeeper, Betsy Head. Mrs. Head's daughter was left only $5.00 from the combined wills because she married a gardener from the estate. The estate is now Hecksher Park, named after August Hecksher who donated $250,000.00 to New York State so it could be purchased as a State Park.

Inisfada, the Nicholas Brady mansion in Manhasset (now St. Ignatius Retreat House) has beautifully carved nursery rhymes etched in the mansion exterior. Ironically, Mrs. Brady, who could not have any children, had an interest in fairy tales. "Inisfada" is Gaelic for "Long Island".

Scenes from "Crocodile Dundee II" were filmed at Eagles Nest the W.K. Vanderbilt mansion in Centerport, now the Vanderbilt Mansion and Planetarium.

Hempstead House, now a part of Sands Point Preserve in Sands Point, was built by railroad tycoon Howard Gould and eventually bought by mining magnate Daniel Guggenheim. When Guggenheim purchased the estate, they did not even have to go through the expense of changing the "G"'s in the gates, house linen or silverware which were all included in the sale of the estate.

Socialite, Bettie Fleischmann Holmes, whose family founded Fleischmann's Yeast Company back in 1896, resided at her Sands Point estate, *The Chimneys*. This was one of the first mansions to utilize the basement for recreation including a bowling alley, nightclub, squash court and theater. The home on two of the original forty acres was up for sale in 2004 for $4.95 million and the estimated taxes were $28,000.00 per year

The horse head in the bed scene from "The Godfather" was filmed at *Falaise*, the Guggenheim estate in Sands Point.

The Guggenheim family members were big investors in aviation.

The Swan Club in Glenwood Landing was originally named *Brook Corners*, the home of Arthur Williams, who was associated with the New York State Department of Water Works. The property was later owned by Benjamin Stern, founder of Sterns Department Store.

Charles Lindbergh, who started his Trans-Continental flight from Roosevelt Field on Long Island, wrote his book <u>We</u> during a stay with the Guggenheim's at their Sands Point estate *Falaise*. Lindbergh also retreated there with his wife after the tragic death of their son.

Falaise, in Sands Point, was home to Harry, son of Daniel Guggenheim and his wife, Newsday founder, Alicia Patterson Guggenheim. Mrs. Guggenheim was the daughter of Joseph Medill Patterson, then owner of the Daily News.

Falaise – Sands Point

The Phipps Administration Building of the Great Neck South Middle and High Schools, now occupies *Bonnie Brink*, the former 30-room mansion of philanthropist and partner in U. S. Steel, Henry Phipps and his wife Amy Phipps. Mr. Phipps died at this estate in 1913.

Falaise – Sands Point

Deepdale Golf Course in North Hills was once part of *Tullaroan*, 198-acre estate of Joseph Peter Grace and his wife Janet MacDonald. Joseph Peter was the son of W.R. Grace, president of the trading and shipping line family.

Otto Keil Florist utilizes the old *Oheka* greenhouses and a real estate office occupies the gatehouse in Cold Spring Harbor.

The Renaissance Country Club and Christopher Moreley Park in North Hills were once a part of *Salamis*, the estate of industrialist John Dennis.

Holland House, former estate of Maxwell Stevens and *The Netherlands*, estate of William S. and Kate Hofstra now make up the Hofstra University campus in Hempstead. The Hofstra mansion was the first college building on the campus.

The Village Club at Sands Point was originally the Isaac Guggenheim estate, *Villa Carola*. Isaac's brother Solomon, benefactor of the Guggenheim Museum, bought the estate at auction for $610,000.00 in 1922 and renamed it *Trillora Court*.

The Manor House – Glen Cove

Since 1967, *The Manor House*, the former mansion of attorney and Standard Oil executive, John Teale Pratt Sr., has been the Harrison Conference Center at Glen Cove.

Joseph Peter Grace of *Tullaroan* purchased the Cornelius F. Kelley estate, *Sunny Skies*, in North Hills, and donated the property and it is now The Convent of Our Lady of Grace Montessori Center. C. F. Kelley was President of the Anaconda Copper Mining Company for 20 years until 1940.

Hempstead House – Sands Point

Katherine Clemmons Gould, wife of Howard Gould of *Hempstead House* in Sands Point, was named defendant in a large number of lawsuits involving top dressmakers of the day because of non-payment. Mr. Gould claimed he could not afford his wife's extravagant jewelry and clothing shopping sprees but in 1907 he was ordered by the court to pay.

The Seventh Day Adventist Offices in North Hills was once *Groombridge*, the estate of John Milburn.

Dowling College in Oakdale was once *Idle Hour*, the home of William K. Vanderbilt Sr. and Alva Vanderbilt. W.K. Sr. was grandson of Commodore Vanderbilt.

Idle Hour - Oakdale

Frank Munsey purchased the Louis Sherry mansion, *Sherryland* (now the Strathmore-Vanderbilt Country Club), in 1922. Munsey had amassed 663 acres and at the time of his death in 1925, Munsey had no heirs and willed his entire estate to the Metropolitan Museum of Art in Manhattan. The Museum developed a model community and the streets were named after American artists.

The old Herbert Lee Pratt estate, *The Braes*, in Glen Cove, was used for filming the Wayne residence in the "Batman Forever" movie.

The Braes – Glen Cove

Harbor Hill is said to have been built on the second highest point on Long Island and was twice the size of the principality of Monaco.

Garden Fountain - Idle Hour – Oakdale

During WWI, *Idle Hour* in Oakdale was not used at all, so W.K. Vanderbilt ordered the lawns of the estate plowed up and potatoes planted to help with the war effort. When the war was over, the grounds were restored to perfection.

Gertrude Vanderbilt Whitney (of *The Manse* in Old Westbury) never cared for high society and devoted much of her time to art. Frustrated by the reluctance of American museums to take work of contemporary artists seriously, she opened the Whitney Museum of Art in 1930.

Frederick Bourne, the President of the Singer Sewing Machine Company, had his 100-room mansion, *Indian Neck Hall*, on 1,000 Oakdale acres the present site of St. John University. St. John's utilizes the estate as its Oakdale campus. It is said that when the house was sold to each owner, it was stipulated that an oil painting of Bourne's son who drowned in the indoor pool, remain in its original spot over the living room fireplace.

Indian Neck Hall - Oakdale

Some scenes from the movie "Less Than Zero", were filmed at Christopher Morely Park, the old Ryan estate, *Salamis*.

Indian Neck Hall boathouse - Oakdale

The New York Institute of Technology – Old Westbury Campus once contained portions of five estates. The campus now only has portions of three:
The Isaiah Burden Residence
White Eagle, the duPont residence
And part of the William Collins Whitney estate

Entrance Indian Neck Hall - Oakdale

Poplar Hill – Glen Cove

Frederick B. Pratt's former residence, *Poplar Hill* in Glen Cove is now the Glengariff and Poplar Hill Nursing Home.

Bailey Arboretum, once known as *Munysunk,* on Bayville Road and Feeks Lane in Lattingtown, was the former estate of Mr. & Mrs. Frank Bailey. Mr. Bailey made his money in the patent business.

Inisfada - Manhasset

The Manhasset mansion of Nicholas Brady, *Inisfada*, was said to have been the fourth largest private residence in 1920 and cost over $6,000,000.00 to furnish. In 1937 there was an auction of the contents that realized only $400,000.00 for Mrs. Brady's charities. Mr. Brady was director of twenty companies and President of New York Edison Company.

The one time President of General Electric resided at his estate, *Portledge*, now the home of Portledge Lower School in Locust Valley.

The AHRC Center in Old Westbury occupies the former James Norman Hill estate, *Big Tree Farm*. J.N. Hill was a railroad executive, financier and son of railroad magnate, James J. Hill. Newspapers of January 1922, stated that J.N. was the leader, with other heirs, in disputing his parents' will and the appointment of the head of the empire by saying that their mother was not of sound mind.

Killenworth was originally the home of George duPont Pratt and now is the Soviet Diplomat Retreat in Glen Cove. The group had first leased J.P. Morgan's house before purchasing *Killenworth*.

Masquetux, the estate of Equitable Life Assurance Company founder, Henry Hyde and *Ardmore*, the Thomas C. Adams Jr. estate, were merged to form the current Southward Ho Country Club in Bayshore.

An admirer of heiress and sculptor Gertrude Vanderbilt Whitney is said to haunt the water tower of their Old Westbury estate, *The Manse*, after he jumped to his death after she did not show for the unveiling of a (nude) statue he created of her. Rumor has it that the statue still remains, boarded up, somewhere on the former estate grounds, now parts of NYIT campus and Old Westbury Golf and Country Club.

The Armour-Ferguson estate, named *The Monastery*, in Huntington, was said to have childrens' gravestones from Europe imported for flooring. Julianna Armour-Ferguson also had much of the mansions' artwork imbedded right into the thick cement walls.

Harbor Hill estate in Roslyn was the site of the $1.5 million dollar reception for England's wildly popular 30-year-old Prince of Wales in 1924. James Abercrombie Burden (of Burden Iron Works), turned over his Syosset estate (*Woodside,* now the Woodcrest Country Club) to the Prince to use as his residence during his 23-day visit.

Knollwood Ruin – Muttontown

The remains of *Knollwood*, the 62-room mansion of Wall Street tycoon, Charles I. Hudson, and then King Zog of Albania, can be found in what is now known as, the Muttontown Preserve (off Route 106). All that remains is the garden facade with fountain, a dual staircase and garden buildings, all of which are in the process of nature reclaiming its own.

The Manor House, once the mansion of John Teale Pratt Sr., was used for location shooting for "Sabrina", "North By Northwest" and "Where's Poppa". The original sports casino is now the Glen Cove YMCA.

At 85 Bayville Avenue in Bayville stands *Callendar House*, the one-time estate of the heir of Charles Broadway Rouss, New York mercantile magnate Peter W. Rouss. Mr. Rouss' father, Charles Broadway was said to have "sham" marriages with other women who filed against his estate after his death.

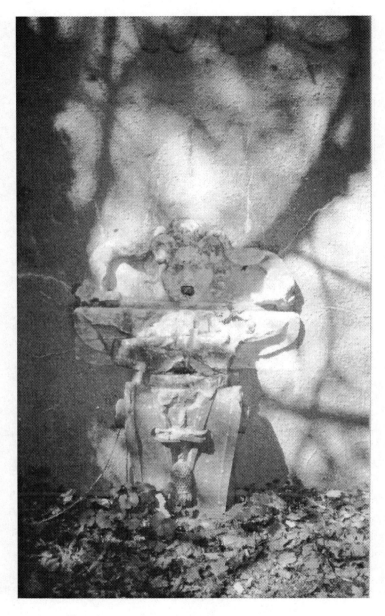

Knollwood Fountain Ruin – Muttontown

For three years, during WWII, *Bonnie Brink,* the Phipps estate in Great Neck, was home to 30 children from London under the care of Lady Brady.

Both George C. Lorillard, tobacco tycoon, and entrepreneur and philanthropist William Bayard Cutting, lived on West brook Farms, now known as Bayard Cutting Arboretum in Great River.

Mrs. Ailsa Mellon Bruce was said to be the richest woman in the world when she owned *Woodlands*, her estate in Syosset (known now as the Town of Oyster Bay Golf Course) and every time Gulf Oil went up a point, her net worth increased.

Sagamore Hill, the Theodore Roosevelt summer White House, was built at a cost of $16,975.00 in 1884 and is now Sagamore Hill National Park in Oyster Bay.

Laurelton Hall Ruins – Laurel Hollow

A single tower with blue stained glass remains from the Lewis Comfort Tiffany estate, *Laurelton Hall.* It can be seen from across Cold Spring Harbor. The house was destroyed by fire in 1957, but the tower along with a few auxiliary buildings can be found near Laurel Hollow Road, in Laurel Hollow.

Mallow – Oyster Bay

Chicago-born financier, Walter Farwell, and his wife Mildred Williams, Chicago Tribune correspondent, had an Oyster Bay estate named *Mallow,* that is now the home of the East Woods School on Yellow Cote Road.

Julianna Armour Ferguson, Armour Meat Company heiress, built her 40-room Spanish castle *The Monastery,* overlooking Huntington Harbor. It was used for the filming of the movie "A Brand Of Cowardice" and the 1916 version of "Romeo and Juliet".

Remains of Monastery – Huntington Bay

Woodland, the estate of wealthy Louisiana planter Bradish Johnson, is now the Hewlett School of East Islip on Suffolk Lane.

In the 1941 Orson Wells classic "Citizen Kane", *Oheka* served as the home of Charles Foster Kane. Aerial views of the mansion were used.

Muttontown Meadows - Muttontown

Muttontown Meadows, former home of Wall Street partner, Edgar Leigh Winthrop, today has an unknown future. It was home to Friends of Long Island's Heritage until recently.

The Islip Art Museum on Irish Lane in Islip was the former home of millionaire businessman Harry K. Knapp until the 1920's. *Brookwood Hall*, as it was known, was also home to the Brookwood Hall Orphanage for 23 years.

Muttontown Meadows on Muttontown Road in Syosset was once the home of Edgar L. Winthrop Jr., of the Wall Street firm, Sampson & Winthrop. Winthrop represented John Jacob Astor III after the senior Astor's will was re-opened because he was killed on the Titanic four months before his son's birth. John III only received a statutory percentage while Vincent, his half brother, of Sands Point, received the bulk of the $159,000,000.00 estate. John III went to court himself in 1959 to fight his half brother Vincent's will. Since Vincent had no children, John III was his only blood relative however he was not left a cent.

Ormston House in Lattingtown and *Old Westbury House* in Old Westbury are examples of the small number of original estates that remain today undivided.

Oheka Indoor Pool – Cold Spring Harbor

Despite protests in London, William Roberson Coe purchased the Carshalton Gates, which were created in 1712 and considered the finest examples of 18th century wrought iron work. Coe purchased the gates for his Brookville estate entrance in 1921. The gates recently underwent a million-dollar restoration and are considered to be the oldest entry gates in America.

The country house of Herbert Lee Pratt, *The Braes*, is now the Webb Institute of Naval Architecture on Crescent Beach Road in Glen Cove. One of the rooms of the mansion was dismantled and moved to Amherst College, alma mater of the Pratt family.

The Marjorie Merriweather Post home in Brookville, was built with angled rooflines to create the look of a small English hamlet. Since 1947 the 178-acre estate, has been the home of the C.W. Post College Campus of Long Island University.

Alfred duPont of *White Eagle* in Old Westbury, was the grandson of the founder of the E.I. duPont Company. Alfred divorced his wife and married his second cousin Alicia, resulting in family bitterness. He also sued members of his own family for slander. When his cousin Thomas ran for United States Senate in 1916, Alfred acquired several Delaware papers and had editorials printed, which contributed to Thomas' defeat.

Workers spent two years piling dirt to build up the foundation of *Oheka* in Cold Spring Harbor to build what Kahn requested, a house to tower over the rest of Long Island.

The W. Serring Howe estate, *Highpool*, is now the Lutheran High School Association on Brookville Road in Brookville.

Oheka castle in Cold Spring Harbor derived its name from it's owner name <u>O</u>tto <u>H</u>erman <u>Ka</u>hn. When Mr. Kahn died in 1934, the services were conducted in the majestic drawing room of the mansion.

Oheka – Cold Spring Harbor

F. W Woolworth, of *Winfield Hall* in Glen Cove did not introduce merchandise exceeding the cost of ten cents into his stores until 1932.

The Floyd family built an estate in Mastic and was occupied by eight generations including William Floyd, a signer of the Declaration of Independence.

A Lattingtown mansion was the star of the movie the "Money Pit".

Meadowcroft, now Roosevelt County Park at Soucci Lakes Preserve in Sayville was owned by investment banker, cousin and legal advisor to Theodore Roosevelt.

The playhouse of Nedinia Hutton remains on the old estate of her parents, which is now the C.W. Post campus. Nedinia changed her name to Dina Merrill, so as not to embarrass her family, when she persued a career in acting.

William Collins Whitney owned ten homes in various locations including Manhattan, Manhasset, South Carolina and the Berkshires.

Nedina's Playhouse – Brookville

Miss Alice De Lamar, daughter of eccentric Captain Joseph De Lamar and heiress to millions and the 55-acre Glen Cove estate, *Pembroke*, refused to exchange it for a Royal Palace. In 1922 she turned down the proposal of Prince Carol of Rumania. The reason for this was a stipulation in her father's will, stated that she could not in any event, forfeit any sum of her inheritance, to her husband therefore she chose to wait for love.

Pembroke estate entrance – Glen Cove

Post Estate – Brookville

The 305-acre campus of C.W. Post College in Brookville is made up of four individual estates: the Marjorie M. Post/Hutton residence is now the Administration Building, the Robinson / Gossler / Hutton Residence is now the Fine Arts Center, and the William E. Hutton Residence is now Lorber Hall.

Woodside, the Burden estate in Syosset, was re-named *Woodside Acres* when it was used to raise cows and sell milk. *Woodside* became *Woodside Acres* when Mrs. Florence Adele Sloan Burden married Richard M. Tobin. Mr. Tobin was a philanthropist and Mrs. Tobin was the great-granddaughter of Commodore Cornelius Vanderbilt.

Mrs. William Woodward Jr. was accused of shooting her husband at their Oyster Bay Cove estate, *The Playhouse*, on October 29, 1955. Although acquitted, some doubted her innocence and she eventually committed suicide in 1976 after the release of a book disclosing little known information regarding the incident.

The marble staircase at *Templeton* was installed after being removed from the Fifth Avenue mansion of Mr. and Mrs. Frederick Guest. The Guest's bought *White Eagle* from the duPont's and re-named the estate *Templeton* and since 1972 it has been the deSeversky Center in Old Westbury.

Marble staircase—Templeton—Brookville

Mott mansion – Bellport

The Bellport Playhouse, in Bellport, was originally part of the 21-acre estate of J.B.L. and Lucy Mott.

Cold Spring Country Club is made up of the 18-hole golf course and stables of *Oheka*, which also had a working farm, dairy, airstrip, and racetrack. A private railroad spur station was originally built to bring construction supplies to the site and subsequently was used for the family and their guests.

The Cushing sisters of Boston were celebrated by high society and renowned in the 1930's and 1940's for their marriages into the most prominent families in the country. The oldest sister, Minnie, married wealthy real estate owner, Vincent Astor, and resided in Sands Point. Betsy married Jock Whitney and made their home *Greentree,* in Manhasset. Barbara (Babe) married Stanley Mortimer Jr., of the Standard Oil family, and then after a divorce, married William S. Paley, CBS founder, and settled in at his estate in North Hills.

Ann, Kevin and Derek at the Knollwood Ruins – Muttontown

Central Park creators, Olmsted Brothers of Brookline Massachusetts, landscaped many of the Long Island estates, and after Massachusetts, Long Island had the highest concentration of Olmsted Brothers projects.

William Randolph Hearst purchased the 81-acre Alva Vanderbilt-Belmont Estate, *Beacon Towers* in 1927 for $400,000.00.

Willow Close was once the Babylon home of George Brownlie on East Neck Road South. The Long Island Yacht Club now occupies the mansion.

The yellow stucco half-timbered Tudor building that is now Harmony Heights School for Girls was the former residence of lawyer John A. Carver of the *Wrexleigh* estate in Oyster Bay.

Clock Tower Remains – Pratt Oval - Glen Cove

Now the Mill River Club, *Appledore,* as the estate was known, was the home of the Vice President of Morgan Guarantee Trust Company, Henry P. Davison, and is adjacent to Coe Hall in Oyster Bay.

Sagamore Hill Historic Park in Oyster Bay contains the summer White House of Theodore Roosevelt and also contains the mansion, *Old Orchard*, built for his son and wife Eleanor.

Marjorie Merriweather Post resided in Brookville and became heir and CEO of Post Cereal which went on to become General Foods and eventually Kraft Foods. Mrs. Post expanded the company by adding Maxwell House Coffee and Jell-O gelatin.

The widow of the president of the New York Gas and Light Company, Sarah Sampson Adam, resided at *Hillside* in Oyster Bay. The house is now the center of a townhouse development known as Colony at Oyster Bay.

Two demolition companies were hired to demolish the Ferguson castle, *The Monastery,* in Huntington. The first one went bankrupt in 1970 trying to knock down the three to four feet thick walls. The stucco gatehouse still remains, as a private residence, at the foot of what seems to have been the main drive on East Shore Road.

Alva Vanderbilt Belmont used her Sands Point castle as one of the meeting places for the suffragette movement. She pursued votes for women with as much vigor as she had to climb the social ladder.

Newly acquired wealth required instant estates. Farms, open fields and rocky shoreline were transformed into tennis courts, spas, swimming pools, golf courses and boathouses. Mature plantings were also planted to make the estates look as if they had been there for years.

The Standard Oil Pratt Family had a family compound in Glen Cove. The Pratt Oval Administration Center survives today as a warehouse at the end of Chestnut Street.

There is a clock tower in the yard of a house nearby and this was once the center of the stable casino building. In it's heyday, the estate employed over 400 employees.

Pratt Oval Remains – Glen Cove

Hempstead House in Sands Point was used in the filming of "Rain Without Thunder", "Running On Empty", and "Great Expectations".

Welwyn – Glen Cove

Welwyn Preserve in Glen Cove was once the estate of Harold Irving Pratt, named *Welwyn*. The word "welwyn" is Welsh for "happiness". Massive tulip trees lined the original main drive and these trees were once used by native Long Islanders to build canoes. The Prince of Wales, (later named the Duke of Windsor), arrived by water and landed off this estate to start his 23-day stay on Long Island in 1924.

Browns Road in Huntington was named after George McKesson Brown, owner of *West Neck Farms.*

Mill Neck Manor School for the Deaf in Mill Neck was once the *Mill Neck Manor* estate of Mr. & Mrs. Robert L. Sefton Dodge. Mrs. Dodge was president of the Harriet Hubbard Ayer Company. At the annual Apple Festival every October the school is open to the public for viewing.

Sefton Manor – Mill Neck

Scenes from "Malcolm X" (1991) and "Scent of A Woman" (1992) were filmed at *Hempstead House*, the old Guggenheim estate in Sands Point.

Lathrop Brown, heir to his father's New York real estate firm, went on to become a member of Congress and then special assistant to the Secretary of the Interior. He decided that Nissequoque was where he wanted his Long Island country home, *Land of Clover.* The estate is now the home of The Knox School.

Alva Vanderbilt coerced her seventeen-year old daughter, Consuelo into a marriage to the Duke of Marborough to gain a royal title in the family. Alva made death threats against Consuelo's sweetheart on several occasions so the Royal marriage could take place. When that marriage was annulled in 1926, it made the newspapers because Alva testified to what she had done to make the marriage happen. Consuelo went on to marry pioneer French aviator and businessman, Colonel Louis Jacques Balsan, and they resided at *Oldfields* which is now the Pine Hollow Country Club off Route 25A in East Norwich.

West Neck Farms - Huntington

The heating and air-conditioning systems at *West Neck Farms* (now part of Coindre Hall County Park in Huntington), used vents below the planters on either side of the mansion entrance to draw in air.

The Howard C. Brokaw estate, *Chimneys*, has been The Muttontown Golf and Country Club on Route 25A in East Norwich since 1960.

Cornelius Vanderbilt Whitney, of Wheatley Hills was the co-founder of Pan American Airways and was a big investor in aviation.

The Manse, the Vanderbilt-Whitney estate in Old Westbury was the setting for the highly publicized custody battle of Gloria Vanderbilt.

The Old Middleton S. Burrill estate, *Jericho Farms*, in Jericho is now the Meadowbrook Golf Club on Cedar Swamp Road.

Congressman, and then later Secretary of the Treasury, Ogden Livingston Mills, with his wife resided in what is now the Woodbury Country Club on Jericho Turnpike in Woodbury. Mr. Mills also ran for Governor of New York in 1926, but lost.

Since 1962, and until recent years, the former home of vivacious Cleveland Standard Oil heiress, Flora Payne Whitney Tower, was part of New York Technology campus in Brookville. The town approved a sub-division for the site and the mansion was then demolished.

Andrew W. Mellon purchased the old 121-acre Morawetz estate in Woodbury for his only daughter Ailsa and her husband, David Bruce, as a Christmas present in 1927. The Bruce's only daughter, Audrey, disappeared with her husband after their small plane was lost over the Caribbean. *Woodland* survives today as The Town of Oyster Bay Public Golf Course off of Southwoods Road.

Two enormous beech trees were moved from Mrs. Coes' father's estate in Massachusetts, but only one survived and remains at The Coe Hall Arboretum in Brookville.

Christian Fellowship Home on Split Rock Road in Syosset was once *Cottsleigh*, the 73-room home of lawyer Franklin B. Lord.

In 1949, 40-room *Sefton Manor* on 86 Mill Neck acres was sold for $216,000.00.

Cottsleigh - Syosset

Oheka, the Otto Kahn estate in Cold Spring Harbor was modeled after the Chateau Fontainebleau in France at a cost of $11,000,000.00 in 1921.

Westbrook - Oakdale

The entrance hall paneling in *Westbrook Farms*, the 60-room mansion at Bayard Cutting Arboretum, was said to have been purchased by Mr. Cutting from a 300-year old estate while on his travels in Europe. The hall also includes original Tiffany stained glass windows.

Caumsett – Lloyd Harbor

Robert Moses acquired the 1,750 acre Marshall Field estate, *Caumsett*, in Lloyd Harbor with two miles of harbor frontage for a parkway extension and creation of a bridge to Connecticut. This idea was opposed by the surrounding community and the estate is now Caumsett State Park.

In the years between the Civil War and WWII, Long Island residents read like a "Who's Who" of America's turn of the century wealthy and powerful.

Harry Payne Whitney was a financier and his stables included some of the fastest racehorses in the country, one winning the Belmont Futurity of 1929. The stables have been converted for educational use and are now part of New York Institute of Technology campus in Brookville.

J. Stuart Blackton, the father of animation, had his estate *Harbourwood* in Cold Spring Harbor. The estate had the world's largest boathouse to accommodate his 150-foot yacht. The estate eventually fell to ruin and was demolished in 1983 and his pet lion was donated to the Bronx Zoo. Since 1968 the waterfront is a National Wildlife Refuge.

West Neck Farms, the 52-room French Chateau overlooking Huntington Harbor on Browns Road, was the former home of pharmaceutical magnate George McKesson and his wife. The mansion and part of the estate survives today as Coindre Hall County Park. The old servant quarters / garage complex now belongs to the Unitarian Fellowship.

Meadowedge, now the West Sayville Country Club started out as the residence of Anson Wade Hard Jr. and Florence Borne Hard. Florence's father lived next door at *Indian Neck Hall*.

Westbury House – Westbury

The movies "North By Northwest", "Age of Innocence", "To Wong Foo, Thanks For Everything Julie Newmar", "Infinity", "Wolf" and most recently "Cruel Intentions" all contained scenes filmed at Old Westbury Gardens, the former Phipps' estate.

The Cold Spring Harbor Laboratories off of Route 25A in Cold Spring Harbor was once a part of the Charles S. Robertson estate, *Little Ipswich*.

Few remnants of *Harbor Hill*, the McKay estate in Roslyn, still survive. There is a horse and rider statue in front of Roslyn High School. There is a gatehouse at Roslyn and Harbor Hill Roads and the original entrance gate is on Roslyn Road and is now the entrance to Country Estates Swimming Club. The old dairyman's cottage is still standing at 40 Elm Drive and the retaining wall behind 85 and 95 Redwood Drive once supported the main winding drive to the house.

The main floor and grounds of *Inisfada*, the Nicholas Brady estate on Searingtown Road in Manhasset, are open to host social as well as spiritual functions as St Ignatius Retreat House.

Westbury House Love Temple – Westbury

The Knole, the old Martin estate, was used for filming scenes for "Mickey Blue Eyes" and it was used as Claus Von Bulow's mansion in "Reversal of Fortune". In April 2004, *The Knole*, in Old Westbury, was sold and after being in one family for many years is now in the hands of contractors.

Banfi Vintners on Cedar Swamp Road in Old Brookville is open to the public for special functions like formal wine and food tasting. *Ringwood*, was the former estate of Alfred G. Vanderbilt II, who was the youngest President of the Jockey Club and his wife, Margaret Emerson, daughter of Bromo-Seltzer inventor. The pioneer promoter of rayon, Sir Samuel Agar Salvage was the builder and first resident of the 60-room mansion on 127 acres.

In the 1920's, the Lamb family sold 1,500 acres of their Fort Solonga estate to New York State for $400.00 an acre and the land is now known as Sunken Meadow State Park.

William Payne Whitney of Manhasset, died in 1972 playing tennis at his estate, *Greentree,* and was buried in his tennis whites in accordance with his wishes. His estate was the largest estate ever probated in the United States at the time. The estimated value was $178,000,000.00.

Long Island has not forgotten its estates or owners. Their names will go down in Long Island history through street names. Woodward Drive named after William Woodward is in Oyster Bay Cove. Woodland Drive named after the Mellon estate in Syosset. Vanderbilt Drives, Courts and Roads are in many towns across Long Island. August Road runs around on one side of Belmont Park, the former August Belmont estate. Tiffany Road in Laurel Hollow, is named after Louis Comfort Tiffany. Grace Drive in Old Westbury is named after William R. Grace.

The New York Institute of Technology, the U.S. Polo Federation and the Golf and Tennis Club are all on land that once belonged to the Whitney Family.

Clayton, the Frisk estate in Roslyn, contains the unique Milliken - Bevin trellis that was restored by the Roslyn Landmark Society in 1989.

North Shore University Hospital in Manhasset was built on fifteen acres donated by the Whitney / Payson families.

James Beekman initiated the Long Island estate phenomenon in the 1860's when he built *The Cliffs* in Brookville.

The two eagles that sat on top of the original Grand Central Station in Manhattan are now located at the entrance to the grounds of the Vanderbilt Planetarium in Centerport.

Daniel Guggenheim from *Hempstead House* in Sands Point lost his son, Benjamin, on the fatal maiden voyage of the Titanic.

White Eagle – Brookville

The Annual Gold Coast Wine Classic and monthly Epicurean Club Dinner are held at the deSeversky Conference Center at NYIT, once called *White Eagle* in Old Westbury. Alfred duPont named the estate *White Eagle* but when steel magnate Frederick Guest bought the estate in 1923, they renamed it *Templeton*.

Robert Moses had to divert the Northern State Parkway away from a route that would have gone through expensive Westbury estates. The result is called "Objector's Bend" a two-mile bend named after the owners of 26 square miles of northern Nassau County who objected. When the residents saw the beautifully landscaped road, they complained about how they did not have access to the Northern State Parkway.

The first hole on the 11-hole golf course of W.K. Vanderbilt Jr. at *Eagles Nest* in Centerport is on the roof of the marine museum and each hole was named after one of his yachts.

Pablo Picasso's 1905 painting "Boy with a Pipe" sold for $104 million in 2004. This painting was in the private Whitney collection at *Greentree* in Manhasset. This was the highest price paid, to date, for a single painting.

The brick and timber East Gate House of *Idle Hour* still stands at the corner of Montauk Highway and Vanderbilt Boulevard in Oakdale. The East Gate house according to local rumor was the place where the W. K. Vanderbilt Sr. went to sulk when he discovered that his wife Alva was seeing Oliver H.P. Belmont during his absences. The East Gate house then became known as the "Pouting House".

Barbara Hutton, nicknamed the poor little rich girl when she was 15, spent time at several Long Island estate including the now vacant *Winfield Hall* at 77 Crescent Beach Road, her grandfathers estate in Glen Cove and her father's estate in Brookville.

In 1944, *Ormston House*, the John E. Aldred estate in Lattingtown, was sold for $75,000.00 to the Order of St. Basil the Great. Isn't it ironic that monks have taken the vow of poverty in one of the wealthiest zip codes in the United States?

Ormston House Gatehouse – Lattingtown

Sefton Manor, which is now the Mill Neck Manor School for the Deaf in Mill Neck, was used as the location for scenes from the movies "Trading Places" and "Death Wish". The front door is said to be over 500 years old.

Winfield Hall – Glen Cove

Winfield Hall, the Woolworth mansion in Glen Cove, cost over $9,000,000.00 to build in 1917 and in 1975 the estimated taxes were $60,000.00 per year. Three members of the family died at this estate. First, in 1917, Edna Woolworth Hutton committed suicide after learning of her husband's infidelities, then F.W. Woolworth in 1919, followed by his wife, Jessie, five years later in 1924.

Richard J. Reynolds and his wife purchased *Winfield Hall* ten years after the death of original owner F.W. Woolworth. Reynolds was said to have converted the garage into a lab where he first created aluminum foil.

Winfield Hall Garden Pavilion – Glen Cove

The 108-room mansion at *Caumsett*, the Marshall Field estate in Lloyd Neck, had one wing removed to downsize to 65 rooms in 1951 to reduce the tax burden. Mr. Field was President of Fields Enterprises which owned the Chicago Sun Times, World Book Encyclopedia, and Simon and Shuster Publishing.

In 1895, Alva Vanderbilt divorced William K. Vanderbilt of *Idle Hour* in Oakdale to marry Oliver Hazard Perry Belmont. The divorce made front-page news of the day because the settlement stipulated that Alva could marry again during W.K.'s lifetime, but W.K. could not.

Otto Kahn is said to have paid Robert Moses to divert the Northern State parkway well south of his estate. The original plan would have brought the parkway through his Cold Spring Harbor estate golf course.

Beech Avenue in Brookville was the Coe's estate East Drive entrance.

Charles E. Wilson, former President of General Motors, was in debt and sold his parcels of land in Old Westbury to the New York State Department of Public Works. The sale enabled Robert Moses to continue to build the Long Island Expressway, with the stipulation that there be no exits or streetlights for the four-mile stretch built on the purchased land.

It took one full-time employee to gather the flowers from the greenhouse and arrange them in the one hundred vases around *Villa Carola*, the Sands Point estate of Isaac Guggenheim.

Long Island estates also served their county. *Oheka*, the Kahn estate in Cold Spring Harbor, served as training center for WWII radio operators. *Hempstead House*, the Guggenheim estate in Sands Point, served as a Naval Devices Training Center and *Laurelton Hall*, the Tiffany estate in Laurel Hollow, served as headquarters for the Marine Research and the National Defense Research Committee.

Marcus Loew, the film producer and theater owner, once resided and died at *Pembroke* in Glen Cove. All that is left of the estate is the marked entrance gate that leads to an upscale housing development.

Dutch Schultz, the famous gangster and bootlegger is said to have leased the Vanderbilt *Idle Hour* mansion in Oakdale during Prohibition and hid there in 1934.

Entrance Bridge and Gatehouse J. P. Morgan Estate

East Island, off the coast of Glen Cove was once called Morgan's Island and was home to banker J.P. Morgan. The original bridge and some outer buildings still remain. The estate, *Matinecock Point*, was the site of the shooting of Morgan in 1915. The shooter, a war-crazed man claimed that Morgan was responsible for continuation of World War I.

Shelter Rock Road is named after the 1,800-ton boulder, Long Island's largest known boulder and it can be found on *Greentree,* the North Hills estate of the late John Hay Whitney and Betsey Cushing Roosevelt Whitney. The Matinecock Indians once used its sizable overhang for shelter. John Hay Whitney was editor in chief and publisher of The New York Herald Tribune from 1961 to 1966 and was chairman of the International Herald Tribune from 1966 until his death. He also was a major motion picture pioneer and was responsible for bringing "Gone With The Wind" and "Rebecca" to the big screen.

In 1939, street cleaners were frolicking at *Oheka,* when the former mansion of Otto Kahn in Cold Spring Harbor was sold to the City of New York and used as a Sanitation Workers Retreat.

A nine-hole private golf course was created at *Villa Carola*, the Isaac Guggenheim estate in Sands Point in 1922 because he was turned down for membership at nearby country clubs, due to his religious beliefs.

The Glen Cove Municipal Golf Course, Prybal Beach and Stanco Park, in Glen Cove, originally made up two estates. *Bogheid* was owned by of J.P. Morgan's partner William Porter who then passed *Bogheid* on to his daughter Helen Porter Prybal. The other was the *Punkin Hill*, Donald Geddes' estate.

Geddes Estate - Lattingtown

Some of Long Island's mansions were built with rooms so large that an entire Levitt house, made popular in Levittown, would have been be able to fit inside.

Gatehouse – Broad Hollow – Old Westbury

The unique gatehouse at the entrance to the State University of New York – Old Westbury campus was once the entrance to *Broad Hollow*, the estate of F. Ambrose Clark who was associated with the Singer Sewing Machine Company and horse racing.

Alva Vanderbilt Belmont supposedly told Duke Atholl (of Blair Castle in Scotland), "Yours is nicer, but mine is more authentic". Alva was referring to her castle, *Beacon Towers* in Sands Point.

The current home of Villa Banfi Importers in Brookville was once the home of Margaret Emerson Vanderbilt and her second husband Alfred Vanderbilt. Mr. Vanderbilt died in 1915 while on the Lusitania which was torpedoed by a German submarine off the coast of Ireland.

The grandfather of Vincent Astor of Sands Point, John Jacob Astor, was considered America's first millionaire. The fortune he left represented one fifth of the total of all personal wealth in America when he died in 1816 at the age of 92. Vincent's grandmother, Caroline Astor, was the creator and leader of New York's "Four Hundred". The number "Four hundred" came from the number of people she could fit in her Manhattan ballroom.

Long Island farms, open fields and rocky shorelines were transformed into spas, tennis courts, swimming pools, golf courses, and boathouses. The elaborate landscapes included reflecting pools, mature plantings, statuary and green velvet stretching for as far as the eye could see.

MANSIONS TO VISIT

Nassau County Museum of Fine Art
1 Museum Drive
Roslyn, NY
(516) 484-9338
Former Residence of: Childs Frick

•

Westbury Gardens & Mansion,
71 Old Westbury Road
Old Westbury, NY
(516) 333-0048
Former Residence of: John Shaffer Phipps and
Margarita Cecile Grace

•

Planting Fields Arboretum
State Historic Park
Oyster Bay, NY
(516) 922-8600
Former Residence of: William Robertson Coe and
Mai Rogers

Coindre Hall County Park,
Friends For Long Islands Heritage
Browns Road
Huntington, NY
(516) 571-7600
Former Residence of: George and Pearl McKesson
Brown

•

Bayard Cutting Arboretum
Montauk Highway
Oakdale, NY
(631) 581-1002
Former Residence of: George L. Lorillard
William Bayard Cutting and Olivia Murray
Mrs. Olivia Bayard Cutting
Olivia Cutting James

•

Vanderbilt Planetarium & Mansion
180 Little Neck Road
Centerport, NY
(631) 854-5555
Former Residence of: William Kissam Vanderbilt II
and Virginia Graham Fair
And then with his second wife
Rosalind Lancaster Warbuton

Sands Point Preserve.
Friends For Long Islands Heritage
Hempstead House & Falaise
95 Middleneck Road
Port Washington, NY
(516) 571-7900
Former Residence of: Howard Gould
and Katherine Clemmons
Daniel Guggenheim and Florence Schloss
Former Residence of: Captain Harry F.
Guggenheim and Caroline Morton
And then with second wife Alicia Patterson

•

Welwyn Preserve
Holocaust Center of Nassau County
100 Crescent Beach Road
Glen Cove, NY
Museum: (516) 571-8002 Preserve: (516) 571-8040
Former Residence of: Harold Irving Pratt and
Harriet Barnes (until her death in 1969)

•

Bailey Arboretum
Bayville Road and Feeks Lane
Lattingtown, NY
(516) 571-8020
Former residence of: Mr. & Mrs. Frank Bailey

Chelsea at Muttontown Preserve
entrance off of 25A
East Norwich NY
(516) 571-8500
Former residence of: Benjamin Moore, attorney and his wife Alexandra. Mrs. Moore re-married and became Alexandra Moore MacKay and lived there until her death in 1983.

•

Meadowcroft
Middle Road
Sayville, NY
(631) 472-4625
Former residence of: John E. Roosevelt and Edith Hamersly

•

St. Ignatious Retreat House
251 Searingtown Road
Manhasset, NY
(516) 621-8300
Former residence of: Nicholas Brady and Genevieve Garvan

•

Muttontown Preserve
Muttontown Lane
East Norwich, NY
(516) 571-8500
Former residence of: Charles I. Husdon
and wife Sara Kierstde
Mrs. Charles H. Senff
C.S. Macveigh
King Gustav S. Zog of Albania
Landsell K. Christie

•

Caumsett State Park
West Neck Road
Lloyd Harbor, NY
(631) 423-1770
Former residence of: Marshall Field III
and Evelyn Marshall

•

Your support by visiting will help to ensure that they will be there for generations to come.

ISBN 1-41204940-7